THE MEGA
COLORING
BOOK
FOR GROWN-UPS

THE MEGA COLORING BOOK FOR GROWN-UPS

With over 170 designs, including mandalas, fish, flowers, butterflies, vintage and abstract patterns, and tattoos

ARCTURUS

ARCTURUS

© 2015 Arcturus Holdings Limited

ISBN 978-1-78599-002-1
AD004805NT

Manufactured in China

2 4 6 8 10 9 7 5 3 1

Introduction

Beneficial in so many ways, coloring calms the mind, occupies
the hands and is a pleasurable way to relax and unwind.
Contrary to popular belief, it unlocks creativity and helps you
enter a freer state of being.

The Mega Coloring Book for Grown-Ups is packed with
wonderful designs from the worlds of nature and art,
all ready for you to color in. By taking part in
this gentle activity, not only will you de-
stress your mind and body, you will
also produce your own beautiful
artwork to treasure.

1

12/13/15 Delaney Anderson

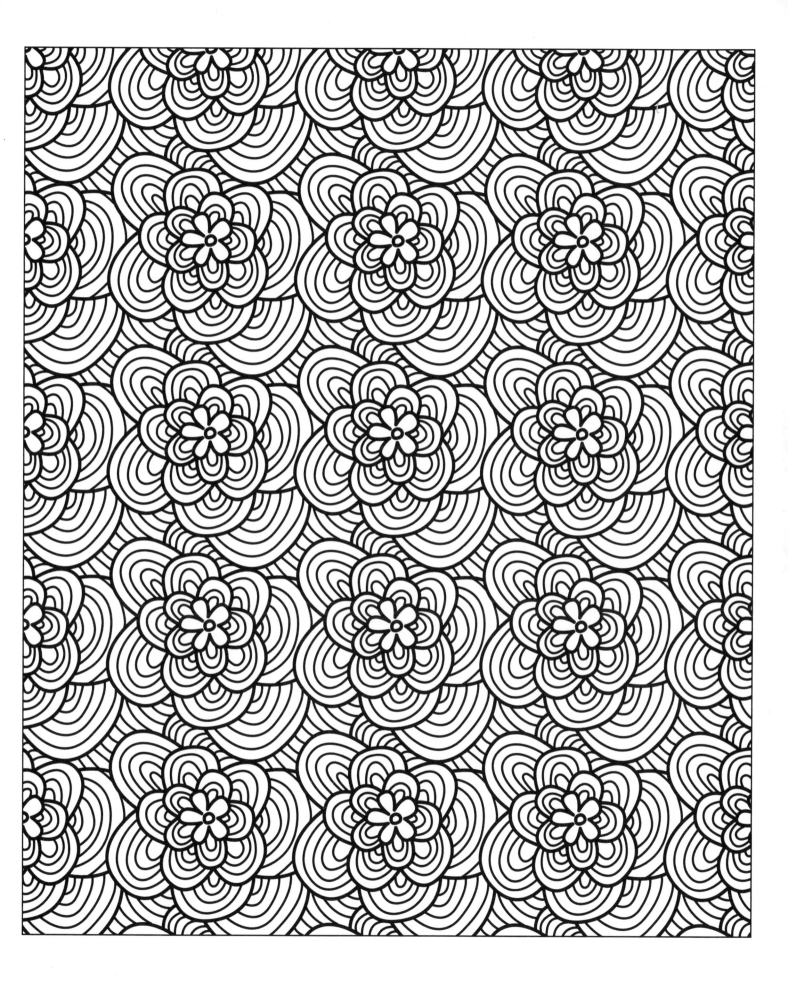

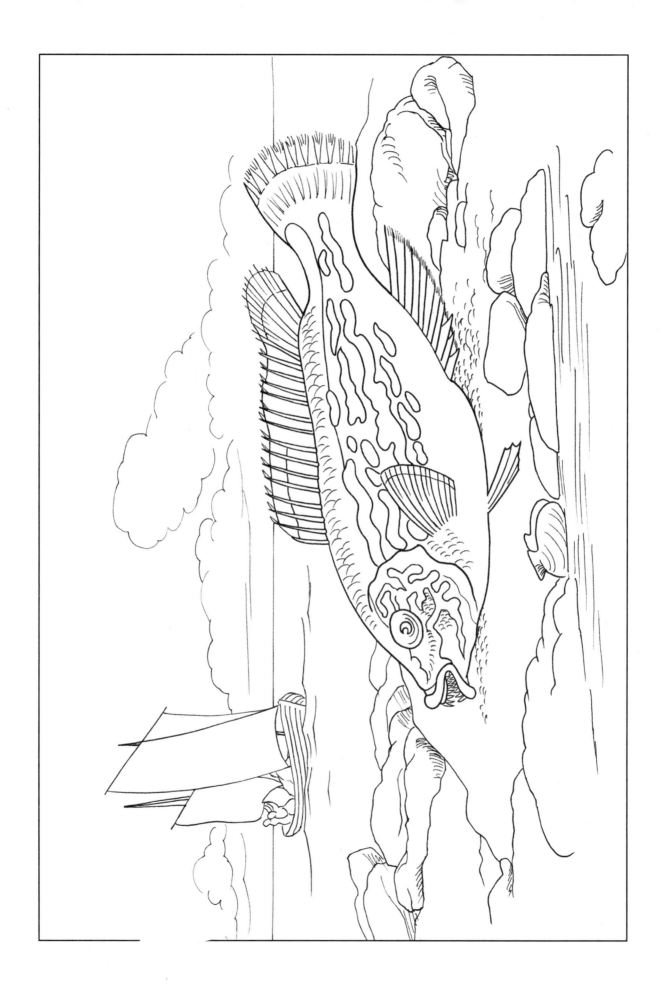

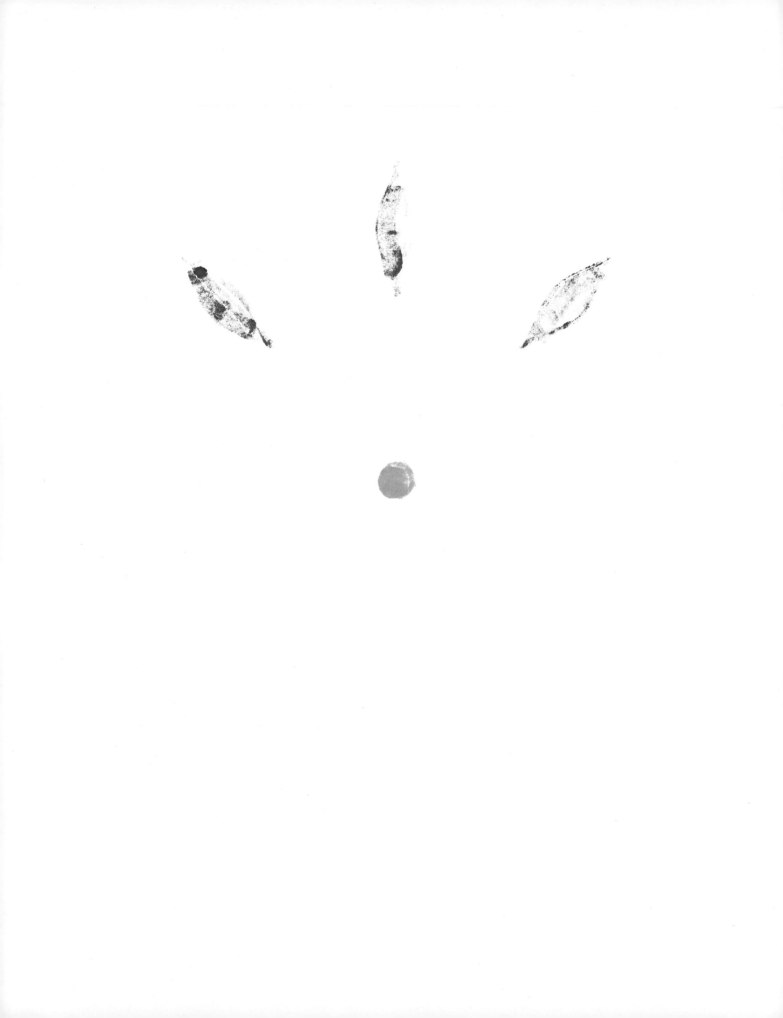

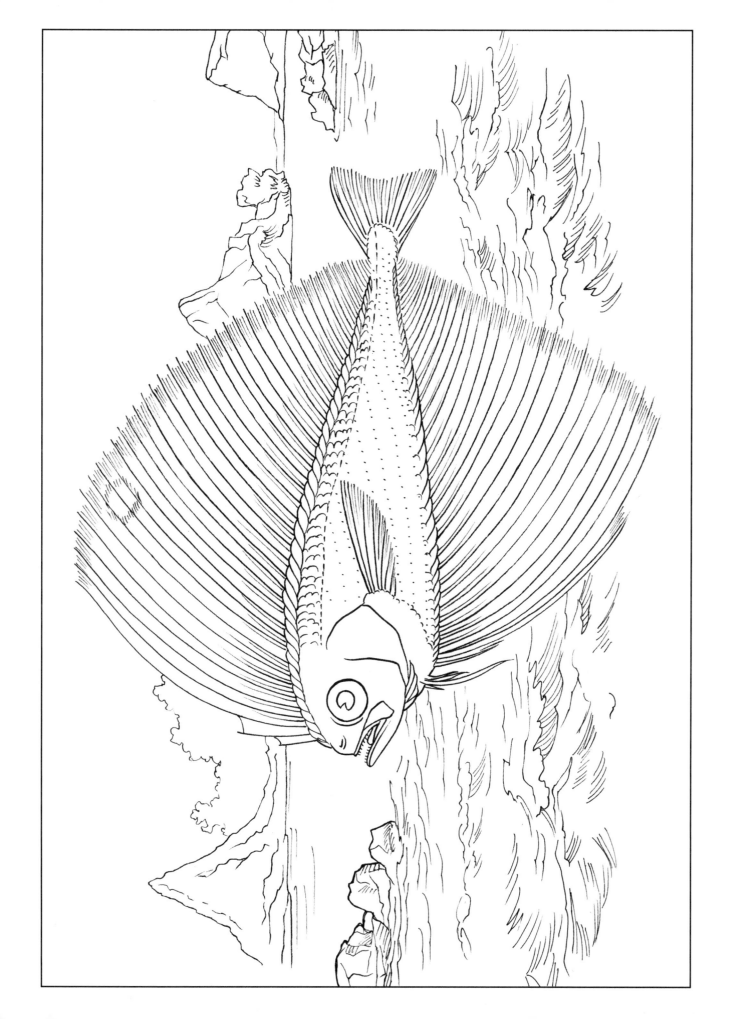

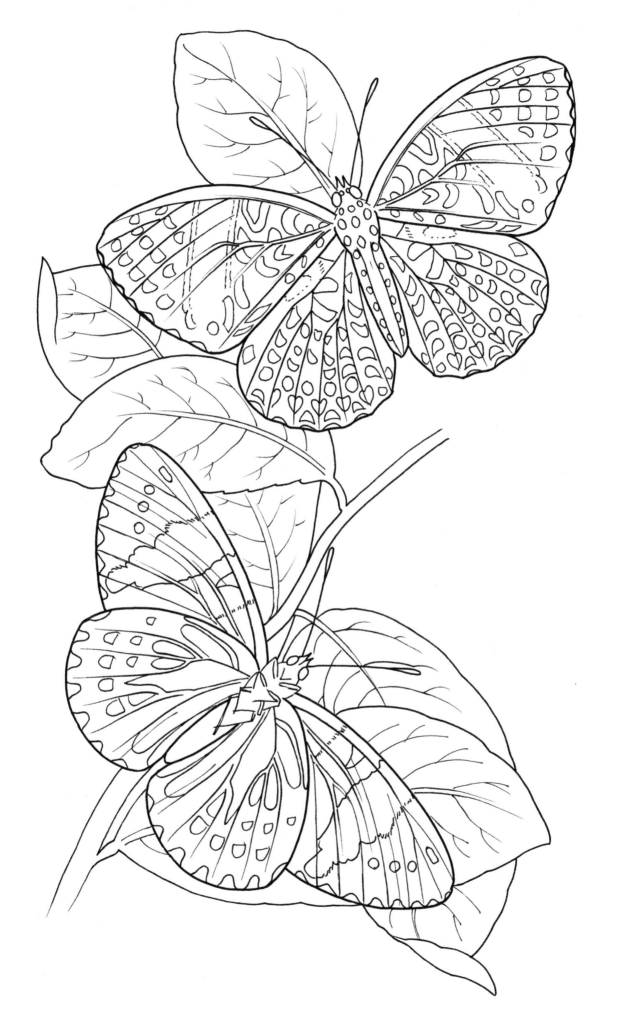

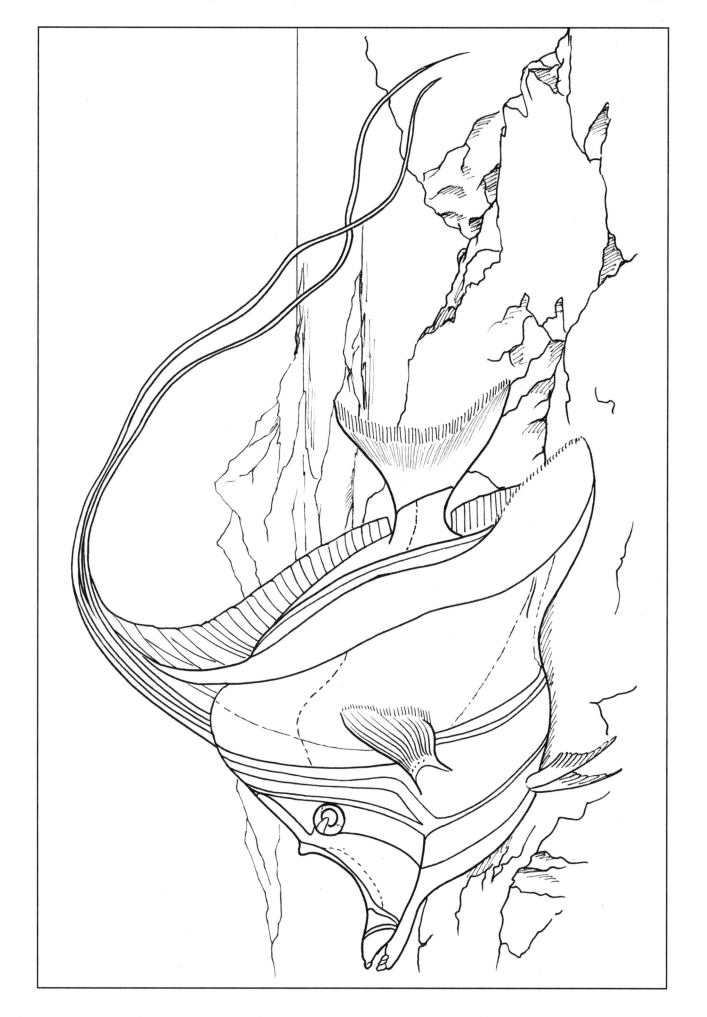

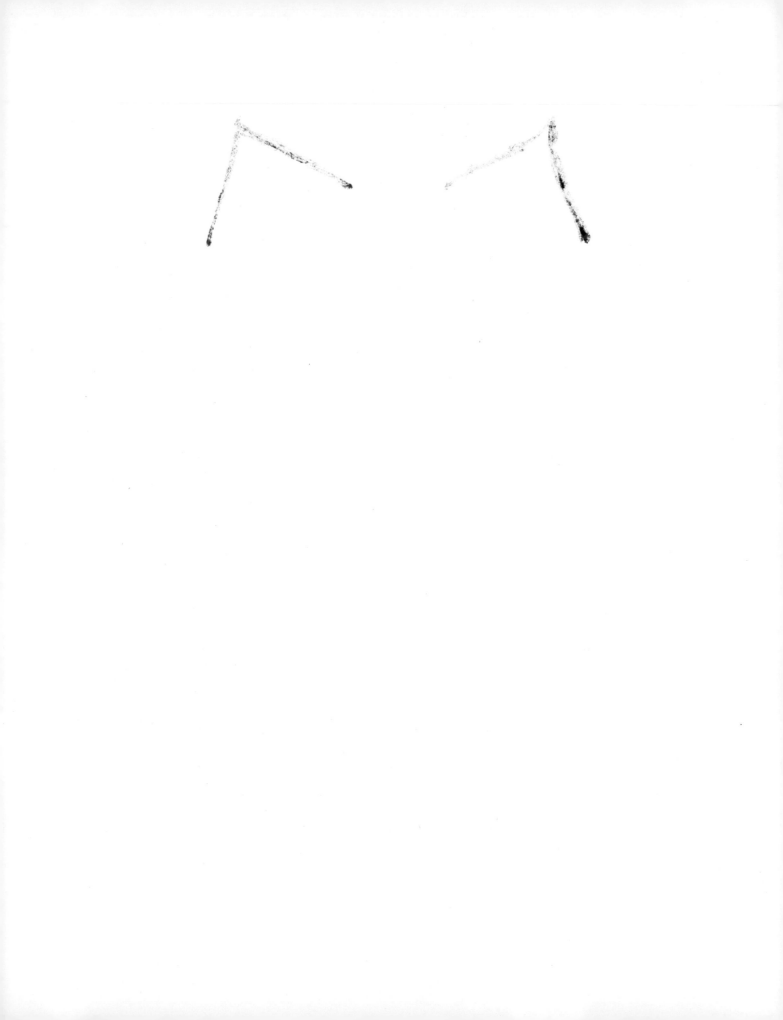

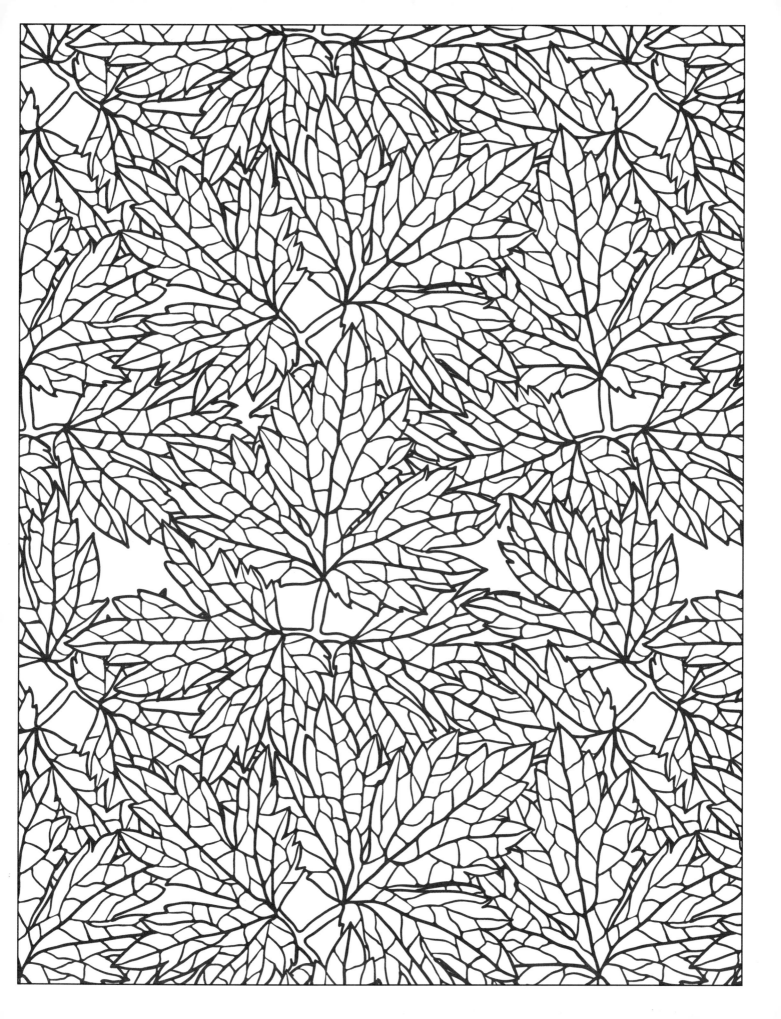